MOVERS,
SHAKERS,
& HISTORY
MAKERS

CHANCE THE RAPPER

INDEPENDENT MASTER OF HIP-HOP FLOW

CONTENT CONSULTANT

AMY CODDINGTON, PhD
ASSISTANT PROFESSOR, DEPARTMENT OF MUSIC
AMHERST COLLEGE

BY JAMIE HUDALLA

CAPSTONE PRESS
a capstone imprint

Capstone Captivate is published by Capstone Press, an imprint of Capstone.
1710 Roe Crest Drive
North Mankato, Minnesota 56003
www.capstonepub.com

Library of Congress Cataloging-in-Publication Data
Names: Hudalla, Jamie, author.
Title: Chance the Rapper : independent master of hip-hop flow / by Jamie Hudalla.
Description: North Mankato : Capstone Press, 2021. | Series: Movers, shakers, and history makers | Includes index. | Audience: Grades 4-6
Identifiers: LCCN 2020001082 (print) | LCCN 2020001083 (ebook) | ISBN 9781496684745 (hardcover) | ISBN 9781496688163 (paperback) | ISBN 9781496684943 (ebook pdf)
Subjects: LCSH: Chance the Rapper—Juvenile literature. | Rap musicians—United States Biography—Juvenile literature.
Classification: LCC ML3930.C442 H83 2021 (print) | LCC ML3930.C442 (ebook) | DDC 782.421649092 [B]—dc23
LC record available at https://lccn.loc.gov/2020001082
LC ebook record available at https://lccn.loc.gov/2020001083

Image Credits
Alamy: Bobby Singh, 26, Diego Corredor/Media Punch, 35, WENN Rights Ltd, 13; AP Images: Rob Grabowski/Invision, cover (foreground); Red Line Editorial: 23; Rex Features: AP/Shutterstock, 39, Chris Pizzello/Invision/AP/Shutterstock, 41, Cindy Barrymore/Shutterstock, 17, Invision/AP/Shutterstock, 28, Koury Angelo/Rolling Stone/Shutterstock, 42, Robb Cohen/Invision/AP/Shutterstock, 20, Scott Garfitt/Shutterstock, 18, Shutterstock, 5, 31; Shutterstock Images: Kathy Hutchins, 8, Kraft74, 10, Losev Artyom, cover (background), 1, Sean Pavone, 6–7, Tinseltown, 25, 36

Editorial Credits
Editor: Charly Haley; Designer: Colleen McLaren

All internet sites appearing in back matter were available and accurate when this book was sent to press.

CONTENTS

CHAPTER ONE
EARLY LIFE.......................................4

CHAPTER TWO
NEW RAPPER ON THE SCENE.........................16

CHAPTER THREE
HIP-HOP HOT SHOT...............................24

CHAPTER FOUR
OUTSIDE OF MUSIC..............................34

CHAPTER FIVE
MOVING FORWARD.............................40

TIMELINE..44
GLOSSARY.......................................46
READ MORE......................................47
INTERNET SITES.................................47
INDEX..48

Words in **bold** are in the glossary.

CHAPTER ONE

EARLY LIFE

Chance the Rapper has always loved music. He was born on April 16, 1993. His real name is Chancelor Jonathan Bennett, but everyone calls him Chance. Chance grew up on the South Side of Chicago, Illinois. His parents usually didn't play music at home. But when they did, they put on cassette tapes of Michael Jackson and disco music. As a kid, Chance usually had a CD player in his hands. His mom wouldn't buy rap music for him because she thought it was inappropriate. But Chance heard rap on the radio, and he loved it.

FAMILY

Chance's family had lived in Chicago for a long time, going all the way back to his great-grandmother. The city was important to Chance and his parents.

When he was a kid, Chance the Rapper could only dream of being onstage at the big concerts he performs at today.

Chicago, Chance's hometown, is the third-largest city in the United States.

Chance's dad, Ken Bennett, wanted to help the city and worked to stop gun violence. Ken's job included helping Chicago's first black mayor, Harold Washington, in the 1980s. He also worked for U.S. president Barack Obama.

Chance's mother, Lisa, worked for the Illinois state government. Her job helped connect community members to the state's law office. Seeing his parents work made Chance want to help people too. He especially wanted to help people in Chicago.

Chance's parents had ideas about the future for Chance and his younger brother, Taylor. Their parents wanted them to go to college and get involved in politics. But the two brothers wanted something different. They loved music so much that they wanted to make their careers out of it.

Chance is close with his family, including his mother, Lisa Bennett (right).

MUSICAL INSPIRATIONS

Chance listened to music whenever he could. He liked Kanye West, Lupe Fiasco, Eminem, Lil Wayne, and other rappers. To Chance, rap music was exciting.

Chance looked up to Eminem. He liked Eminem's verses. But Kanye West was Chance's favorite rapper. West was from Chicago too. When Chance was in fourth grade, his friend's mom gave him one of West's albums. Chance had to hide it from his mom, who didn't approve of rap music. He loved the album because the lyrics made him feel like someone understood him.

Chance has said *Late Registration* is his favorite Kanye West album.

Chance was ready to try writing his own songs. He started rapping when he was in sixth grade. He wanted to make music like West's. At first, he wrote his own lyrics and rapped them to West's beats. Chance's cousin had a music studio. He let Chance use the studio to record **freestyles**. Chance also listened to jazz and gospel music. But rap was still his favorite.

EDUCATION

Chance made a lot of music at Jones College Prep High School. He learned how to play piano, saxophone, and violin. But rapping and singing were still his main focus. In ninth grade, Chance and a friend formed a rap group called Instrumentality. They recorded their music and shared it on YouTube and Facebook. They told friends to share the videos. Soon many people were following them. People loved their music.

OTHER FAMOUS RAPPERS FROM CHICAGO

- CHIEF KEEF
- COMMON
- EARL SWEATSHIRT
- G HERBO
- KANYE WEST
- LIL DURK
- LUPE FIASCO
- NONAME
- TWISTA
- VIC MENSA

Chance showed off his skills at school talent shows. He also went to a Chicago library that had an artists' studio. The library held a contest, and Chance entered a song. He won second place. The man who ran the library's studio loved the song. He said it was the best song about Chicago he had ever heard. He told Chicago's mayor about it.

Mayor Richard M. Daley showed up at the library to see Chance perform. Chance was surprised that the mayor wanted to listen to his song!

Chance rapped at the library's **open mic nights** too. Sometimes he forgot his lyrics. But the crowd still loved him. Hundreds of people came out to watch.

Chance started out by playing shows in Chicago.

Producers came to the shows, on the lookout for new talent. Chance got to know the producers. Soon they gave him opportunities to record his music.

Chance hit a slump during his senior year of high school. He was failing six of his seven classes. His teachers told him he'd never make it as a musician. He started experimenting with drugs. One day, police found Chance with drugs outside of his school. They arrested him and took him to jail. Chance was also suspended from school for 10 days. He had to sit in his dad's office instead. Chance was angry and bored. He thought the suspension wasn't fair. To keep busy, Chance started writing lyrics. The more he wrote, the more he learned about himself. He started feeling better too. He felt like his dream of becoming a rapper could come true.

Chance kept working on music throughout his suspension. By the time he got back to school, he had written the raps for his first **mixtape**. It was called *10 Day*.

WHAT DID CHANCE LIKE TO DO IN SCHOOL?

- HE WON A MICHAEL JACKSON TALENT SHOW IN FOURTH GRADE.

- HE PERFORMED AT TALENT SHOWS IN BETWEEN CLASSES AT HIS HIGH SCHOOL.

- HE JOINED HIS HIGH SCHOOL'S SLAM POETRY CLUB.

Chance's lyrics were about his frustrations with high school. He had written about getting suspended. But he had also written about prom and other high school experiences.

Chance didn't like school, but he knew his parents wanted him to go to college. After high school, Chance tried community college for one week before dropping out. His parents were mad. But Chance had a plan. He was going to make it big in the hip-hop world.

CHAPTER TWO

NEW RAPPER ON THE SCENE

Not long after dropping out of college, Chance started rapping full time. His parents didn't approve of this, so they wouldn't let him live at home. He slept on sofas at his friends' houses. Then one of Chance's friends died. Chance was devastated. He called his parents and told them what had happened. He also told his parents how important music was to him. Chance's parents told him to come home. His dad gave him one year to find success in the music world. If Chance didn't succeed, his dad would encourage him to find a different job. But soon after that, Chance's parents didn't have to worry.

As Chance got more famous, he began rapping at bigger shows.

Chance officially released *10 Day* in April 2012. Though Chance had written the songs during his suspension, the mixtape took about a year to record and produce. He had recorded it in the Chicago library studio. Chance released the completed mixtape online. It got more than 400,000 **downloads** on the music website DatPiff. Chance got a lot of attention after releasing *10 Day*. His dad helped him advertise the mixtape.

Childish Gambino helped Chance get his first big tour.

A magazine wrote that Chance was the next rapper to look out for. Chance's parents grew proud of what their son had accomplished.

10 Day also gained the attention of rapper Childish Gambino. He invited Chance on his North America tour in 2012. They even collaborated on a few songs for Chance's 2013 mixtape *Acid Rap*. Chance's second mixtape was more popular than his first. It got more than one million downloads.

Acid Rap included sad songs about the death of a friend. But it also had many playful songs. Chance was growing up and trying to find his place in the music world. His style had evolved to include gospel and jazzy piano.

After Chance released *Acid Rap*, he got the opportunity to sign with a **record label**. Record labels help artists reach big audiences and become famous. They pay musicians a lot of money and get good studios to record their music. But Chance wanted to keep control over his work. So he didn't sign with the label. He decided to stay **independent**.

By 2013, Chance was playing to huge crowds.

DOING THINGS DIFFERENTLY

Not signing with a label meant Chance could make all of the decisions regarding his music. Chance wanted to make it easier for fans to hear his songs, so he released them all online for free. Most artists want to sell their albums to make more money. But Chance made most of his money by selling tickets to his concerts and selling T-shirts and hats at the shows.

Chance had a lot of fans in Chicago. He performed sold-out shows at small **venues** there. He promoted himself to get more followers. But being independent didn't mean Chance was doing everything by himself. He had a lot of people helping him. His family supported him. Producers recorded his songs. Other rappers collaborated with him.

Chance was proud of doing things his own way as an independent artist. He encouraged other rappers to do the same. As Chance got more involved in the music industry, he made his next big move.

CHANCE'S STYLE

Chance the Rapper doesn't only like to rap. He likes clothing and style too. Chance is known for being youthful and positive, and he often wears overalls to play into this. In 2016, Chance redesigned baseball caps for the Chicago White Sox, one of the city's pro baseball teams. Chance also wears a hat with the number 3 on it. He started wearing the hat when he was working on his third mixtape. But the number 3 has other meanings too. It stands for the three members in Chance's family at that time (himself, his girlfriend, and their first daughter). It also stands for the Holy Trinity, which is a symbol in the Christian religion.

TROUBLE IN CALIFORNIA

In 2014, Chance moved to Los Angeles, California. He lived in a Hollywood mansion with a British singer named James Blake. They called the mansion a castle.

Then James Blake left, and Chance was alone in the big house. Chance struggled with being far away from his home in Chicago. He had become famous and successful. But in some ways the fame was difficult. Chance's mental health suffered. Partying and drug abuse became his way of coping. It was a dangerous path to follow.

Drugs and parties distracted Chance from making music. He couldn't get work done. Chance had written plenty of music in Chicago, but he struggled to write in Los Angeles. Chance soon realized that living in California wouldn't help him reach his goals.

FACT

As Chance became more successful, he started to get work advertising clothes and other products. In 2014, Chance was asked to star in a video advertising pants.

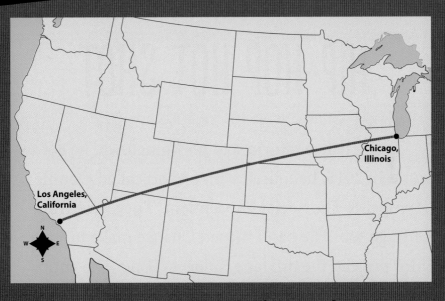

It was hard for Chance to be far away from his hometown. Los Angeles is about 2,000 miles (3,200 kilometers) from Chicago. When Chance lived in Los Angeles, it would have taken him about four hours to fly home to Chicago. It would have taken him about 30 hours to drive.

After six months in Los Angeles, Chance moved back to Chicago. He started making music that was true to himself again. Many of his songs refer to the mistake he made in getting involved with drugs.

CHAPTER THREE

HIP-HOP HOT SHOT

Once Chance returned to his hometown, he got to work. In 2015, he toured with a band called Donnie Trumpet & The Social Experiment. They were from Chicago too. The band helped Chance make his third project, the mixtape *Coloring Book*. The entire mixtape took Chance only about two months to make. He worked so hard that he slept in the studio. His parents visited him to make sure he was okay. But the tough times in Los Angeles were over. Chance had found his flow again.

Chance tried a lot of new things with *Coloring Book*. He collaborated with Kanye West on the mixtape. They had already worked together on West's album *Life of Pablo*. Working with West made Chance even more famous.

Kanye West has worked on projects with Chance.

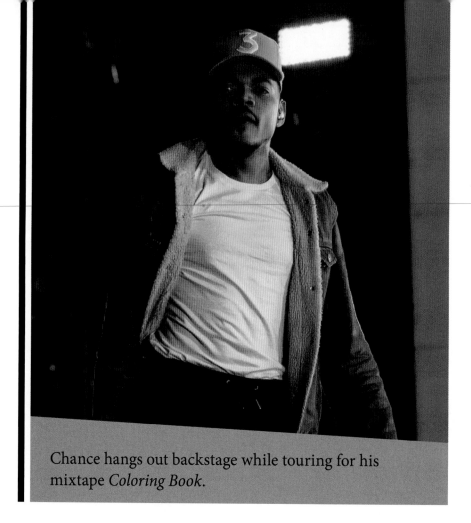

Chance hangs out backstage while touring for his mixtape *Coloring Book*.

Chance also performed a song on *The Tonight Show Starring Jimmy Fallon* in 2016. This gave people a taste of the soulful music on *Coloring Book*. Chance was backed by a choir, trumpets, and guitars as he rapped on TV. Chance's fans tweeted and posted on social media about how great the performance was. Other famous musicians posted about the performance too.

Coloring Book had a lot of positive songs. It gave many people reasons to smile. It reminded people to be grateful and to stay hopeful when life gets hard. After that TV performance, he released *Coloring Book* on Apple Music, an online music **streaming** service. *Coloring Book* was the first streaming-only album to reach *Billboard*'s Top 10 albums list.

Later that year, Chance went on a world tour. It was the first-ever rap tour with a sign language interpreter on staff. Chance wanted everyone to be able to experience his music. He encouraged fans to bring friends who were deaf to the concerts. He performed in 36 cities.

In 2017, *Coloring Book* won Best Rap Album at the Grammy Awards. The Grammy Awards recognize the work of musicians in a wide range of music styles.

FACT

In 2017, Chance headlined Lollapalooza, a music festival in Chicago. He got one of the largest crowds in the festival's history. About 100,000 people showed up.

Chance's album was the first streaming-only album to win a Grammy. Chance won Grammys for Best New Artist and Best Rap Performance that year too.

Several magazines named *Coloring Book* one of the top albums of 2017. People loved Chance's music for its positivity.

Chance gave an acceptance speech after winning a Grammy Award in 2017.

Chance kept his concerts positive too. At one show, he brought the Muppets out onstage. People liked seeing him with these children's TV characters. Song after song, Chance transformed the hip-hop world with his uplifting lyrics and beats. Chance didn't shy away from hard topics in his music. But he found a way to write about them while also sending a message of hope, saying that life can get better.

Throughout 2017, Chance's fame got him many spots on TV shows and in commercials. He hosted an episode of the show *Saturday Night Live*. Because the episode aired around the holidays, Chance opened the show with a funny rap about Thanksgiving. Live turkeys joined him onstage.

FACT

Chance received an Emmy nomination for the song "Last Christmas," which he performed on *Saturday Night Live* in 2017. An Emmy award recognizes a person's success in television.

Chance started to get money from companies like Nike, Nestlé, and Apple for advertising their brands. He starred in their commercials and told people to buy their products. He had allowed Apple to be the only company that could stream *Coloring Book* online. People needed to pay to listen to the mixtape on Apple Music. Apple paid Chance half a million dollars for this. Some people criticized Chance for this deal with Apple. They said it meant Chance wasn't independent anymore. But Chance's deal with Apple had only lasted for two weeks. Then the mixtape became available for free on other sites.

THE LION KING

As Chance became more famous, he started to get opportunities to act in movies. He acted in the funny horror movie *Slice* in 2018. Then he got the chance to help with a remake of one of his favorite childhood movies. It was *The Lion King* movie in 2019. Chance was asked to be the voice of an animal character called "Bush Baby." He also made sound effects for some other animals in the movie and contributed some singing.

Chance is known for keeping his performances fun
and positive.

In 2018, Chance released four new songs. They
were released just in time for his performance at the
Special Olympics, an event at which people with
intellectual disabilities compete in sports. These songs
got fans excited about Chance's next big project.

NOTABLE COLLABORATIONS

Chance the Rapper has worked on songs with many other famous musicians. Some of them are:

- CARDI B
- CHILDISH GAMBINO
- ED SHEERAN
- JUSTIN BIEBER
- KANYE WEST
- MACKLEMORE

THE BIG DAY

Chance released his **debut** album, *The Big Day*, in July 2019. Even though Chance had released three mixtapes, *The Big Day* was considered his first album. Albums are larger projects that take longer to make than mixtapes. Sometimes albums have a theme. *The Big Day*'s theme is love and marriage.

The album reached number two on *Billboard*'s Top 10 list. *The Big Day* features many artists, including John Legend, Shawn Mendes, and Nicki Minaj. It also features Chance's brother, Taylor.

Many of the songs were inspired by Chance's family. He and his girlfriend had gotten married that year, and they had another daughter. The album received many positive reviews. But some fans didn't like it. They felt they couldn't relate to Chance's new music about his family. Many fans wanted Chance the Rapper, not Chance the Family Man. In his life, Chance works hard to balance both of these roles.

CHAPTER FOUR

OUTSIDE OF MUSIC

Chance was nine years old when he met his future wife, Kirsten Corley. They met at his mom's office party. Chance was too scared to talk to her. Eventually, the two became friends. They started dating in 2013. Two years later, Corley gave birth to their first daughter, Kensli. Their baby had an irregular heartbeat. Chance was scared for his daughter. He started praying. He was very protective of Kensli. He didn't post photos of her on social media until nearly two years after she was born.

Chance asked Corley to marry him at a Fourth of July party in 2018. Their wedding happened the next March in Newport Beach, California. Celebrities including Kanye West and Kim Kardashian went to the wedding.

Chance and his wife, Kirsten Corley, in 2018

Sometimes Chance brings his family to events, such as the movie premiere of *The Lion King*. There, he held his daughter, Kensli, as he and his wife posed for a photo.

In August 2019, Chance and Corley welcomed their second daughter, Marli Grace. Chance had planned to tour for his album *The Big Day*. But he wanted to spend more time with his family. So he canceled the tour. Some fans were disappointed. But Chance knew he had made the right decision for his family. Chance says that taking care of kids is more work than he thought it would be. Sometimes Chance travels with his daughters and takes them to the studio with him. Chance has found a way to value family and music in the city he loves, Chicago.

CHRISTIAN INFLUENCE

Chance was raised a Christian by his grandmother, and many of his lyrics reflect this. Chance became more involved with religion after his daughter Kensli was born with a heart defect. *Coloring Book*, which some people consider to be a gospel album, references blessings and angels. In 2018, Chance left the United States by himself to take some time to read the Bible. He often shares his faith on Instagram. However, while Chance identifies as a rapper who is Christian, he says he does not make Christian rap.

HELPING HIS COMMUNITY

Since Chicago had given Chance so much, he wanted to give back to his city. Chance speaks out against gun violence. He uses his fame to tell people about the problem. Many of Chance's lyrics point out Chicago's high crime rates and say that things need to change.

FACT

In 2017, Chance donated $1 million to Chicago public schools.

Chance also helps children in Chicago. He started an organization called SocialWorks that aims to empower kids. SocialWorks hosts fundraisers to help children get health care and warm clothes for the cold winters. It also hosts open mics at schools in Chicago. It encourages kids to get involved in the arts, education, and their communities.

In 2014, Chicago's mayor Rahm Emanuel gave Chance an award for his positive influence on kids. Chance also won the Humanitarian Award at the BET Awards, which celebrates the accomplishments of black Americans in entertainment. The BET award was presented to Chance by his family friend, former first lady Michelle Obama.

Chance works to help homeless people too. In 2016, he started a fundraiser to give coats to homeless people in Chicago. He called the fundraiser the Warmest Winter and bought 1,175 coats with the money he raised.

Chance and former first lady Michelle Obama (left) at a concert in Chicago

In 2017, Chance partnered with former president Barack Obama to promote leadership in young men of color. This program was called My Brother's Keeper Alliance. It pairs young men with adults who can help them work toward their dreams. Just like his parents, Chance found a way to help his community. Some people even wanted him to run for mayor.

FACT

Chance helped create a fashion line called "Thank You Obama" in honor of former president Barack Obama.

MOVING FORWARD

Chance has kept busy with music. He has moved forward with other work as well. In late 2019, a talent agency began working with Chance. The agency began helping Chance organize his opportunities for public speaking, acting, charity work, and more. But Chance's music is still independent.

Chance found time to release a new music video in fall 2019. It was for the song "We Go High," from *The Big Day*. He went on TV shows to talk about the video. The video shows a serious story about Chance facing mistakes from his past. But it ends on a positive note showing Chance meeting his wife.

Chance spoke at a charity event called WE Day California in 2019.

Chance gave a concert in Las Vegas in 2019.

Chance also became a judge on Netflix's *Rhythm + Flow*, a hip-hop competition show. On this show, Chance could help discover young rappers. Not so long ago, Chance was a young rapper trying to get discovered. Now he is an award-winning artist.

Chance has many different interests. He likes rapping and fashion. He wants to help others. As an independent artist, he can take his career anywhere he wants. Fans of Chance the Rapper wait excitedly to see what he'll do next.

TIMELINE

1993: Chance the Rapper is born in Chicago as Chancelor Bennett.

2012: Chance graduates from high school.

2012: Chance releases his first mixtape, *10 Day*.

2013: Chance releases *Acid Rap*.

2013: Chance starts to date Kirsten Corley.

2014: Chance moves to Los Angeles for six months before returning to Chicago.

2015: Chance and Corley have their first daughter, Kensli.

2016: Chance releases *Coloring Book*.

2017: Chance wins three Grammy awards.

2019: Chance and Corley get married.

2019: Chance releases *The Big Day*.

2019: Chance and Corley's second daughter, Marli Grace, is born.

debut (day-BYOO)
the first time
something happens in a
musician's career

**downloads
(DOUN-lohds)**
songs that have been
copied from the internet
onto someone's computer

freestyles (FREE-stiles)
raps with lyrics that are
made up on the spot,
sometimes without music

**independent
(in-di-PEN-duhnt)**
a musician who does not
have a contract with a
record label and owns all
of his or her own music

mixtape (MIKS-tayp)
a collection of songs that
is usually less organized
and lower in quality than
an album

**open mic nights
(OH-pun MYEK NITES)**
live shows where anyone
can perform on stage

**producers
(pruh-DOOS-ers)**
people who record songs
for musicians and help
musicians make albums

**record label
(REK-urd LAY-buhl)**
a company that sells
an artist's music to
make money

**streaming
(STREE-ming)**
listening to music or
watching a video on the
internet

venues (VEN-yoos)
places where organized
events, such as concerts,
are held

READ MORE

Head, Tom, and Deirdre Head. *Kanye West: Conquering Music and Fashion*. New York: Enslow Publishing, 2020.

Niver, Heather Moore. *Chance the Rapper: Hip-Hop Artist*. New York: Enslow Publishing, 2019.

Toth, Henrietta. *Lil Nas X: Record-Breaking Musician Who Blurs the Lines*. North Mankato, MN: Capstone Press, 2021.

INTERNET SITES

Chance the Rapper's Official Website
www.chanceraps.com

Chicagoist, **a News Website Owned by Chance the Rapper**
www.chicagoist.com

SocialWorks, Chance the Rapper's Youth Empowerment Organization
www.socialworkschi.org

INDEX

10 Day, 14, 18–19

Acid Rap, 19
Apple Music, 27, 30

Big Day, The, 32–33, 36, 40, 43
Blake, James, 22

Chicago, Illinois, 4–7, 9, 12, 18, 21, 22, 23, 24, 27, 36–39
Childish Gambino, 19, 32
Christianity, 21, 37
Coloring Book, 24–28, 30, 37
Corley, Kirsten, 34–36

Eminem, 9

Facebook, 11

gospel, 11, 19, 37
Grammy Awards, 27–28
gun violence, 6, 37

Lion King, The, 30
Los Angeles, California, 11, 22–23, 24
lyrics, 9–11, 13–15, 29, 37

Obama, Barack, 6, 39
Obama, Michelle, 38
open mic nights, 13, 38

producers, 14, 21

record labels, 19–20

Saturday Night Live, 29

West, Kanye, 9–11, 12, 24, 32, 34

YouTube, 11